FREEDOM FOR THE CAPTIVES

PEACE·AND·JUSTICE·SERIES **5**

FREEDOM FOR THE CAPTIVES

How Love Is Rebuilding Lives in Spain

JOSÉ GALLARDO

HERALD PRESS
Scottdale, Pennsylvania
Kitchener, Ontario

LIBRARY OF CONGRESS
Library of Congress Cataloging-in-Publication Data

Gallardo, José, 1944-
    Freedom for the captives : how love is rebuilding lives in Spain /
José Gallardo.
        p.   cm. — (Peace and justice series ; 5)
    ISBN 0-8361-3474-5 (pbk.)
    1. Gamonal Community (Gamonal, Burgos, Spain)—History.
    2. Gamonal (Burgos, Spain)—Church history.   3. Burgos (Spain)-
-Church history.   I. Title.   II. Series.
BV4407.6.G35 1988   88-5953
289.7´46353—dc19   CIP

The cover photograph by José Gallardo shows young people from the Christian community in Gamonal speaking with prisoners inside the prison walls.

Except where noted otherwise, Scripture passages are from the *Good News Bible*. Old Testament copyright © American Bible Society 1976; New Testament copyright © American Bible Society 1966, 1971, 1976.

Scripture passages marked RSV are from the Revised Standard Version of the Bible, copyrighted 1946, 1952, © 1971, 1973.

To those whose lives were changed
and those whose lives were used by God
for that purpose

Contents

Foreword

Most societies today face rapid social change and a growing gap between rich and poor. For example, changes in communication have changed how we live, work, relax, and teach values to the young. At the same time, the rich tend to get richer and the poor poorer.

How, then, can we bring about social change in peaceful ways? And how can we solve problems of injustice without violent revolution?

Rapid social change and the growing gap between rich and poor often provide a setting for trouble. Both tend to disrupt family life, destroy traditional values, cause idleness, and foster crime. Some results are drug abuse, theft, rape, and murder. So what is the good news?

As author José Gallardo demonstrates, life can be lived with meaning and purpose, despite such upheavals in society. The key, as he illustrates from his own life, is practicing the love and compassion of Jesus. It is in being a community that redeems persons from a lesser way of life.

In *Freedom for the Captives*, the author shows how God's plan of love and reconciliation can be good news today. The poor can find hope through people who share their wealth. Captives who have lost community through crime and prison sentences can be returned to society as constructive citizens. The brokenhearted can be made whole.

José Gallardo writes out of his own experiences of injustice in Spain, Belgium, and countries of South America. He shows how he found wholeness in the body of Christ. The Christian community in which he now lives and works holds their goods as a group. By combining their material and spiritual resources, they are better able to help others to rebuild their lives and homes.

Freedom for the Captives tells an interesting story of how to rebuild broken lives. As book five in the Peace and Justice Series listed at the back of the book, it offers food for thought and action. For further study, check the references listed there.

—J. Allen Brubaker, Editor
Peace and Justice Series

Introduction

This book will develop the different points of the prophecy announced in Isaiah 61 and restated in Luke 4:18-19. Through the chapters that follow, I will try to share the story of my life during the past ten years. My purpose is to show how biblical principles are real and can be applied to concrete situations today.

It may be that what I have to tell will not be extraordinary. No doubt many could share the same types of experiences and perhaps report better results. This is my testimony of how God's power was manifested in weakness and human need, and in situations that often seemed desperate.

The good news of salvation through Jesus is a powerful agent for social change at all levels. What happens to one person can happen to many others. What occurs in one place can also occur in other places. My purpose is to encourage all who have decided to follow Jesus and to put into practice his teachings of love and nonviolence. These he has given us in the Gospels through his word and his action. It is not just an ideal. It is practical, and the only road we can take. Besides, it is the most effective way. It means doing the will of God as Jesus has demonstrated by his example.

If you do not believe in Jesus as the only Savior of the world but are looking for the truth with a sincere heart, you will not be disappointed. I have put my confidence in him and have not been disappointed. The story of my ten years of experience with Christ is not much. When joined to a similar testimony by many others today and in years past, however, it is worthy of serious consideration.

—*José Gallardo*

FREEDOM FOR THE CAPTIVES

"The Spirit of the Lord is upon me because he has anointed me to preach good news to the poor. He has sent me to bind up the brokenhearted, to proclaim freedom for the captives, and recovery of sight to the blind, to set at liberty those who are oppressed, to proclaim the acceptable year of the Lord."

—Luke 4:18-19; Isaiah 61:1

CHAPTER 1

The Spirit of the Lord Is Upon Me

A Personal Testimony

During the 14 years I lived outside my country, I never imagined that when I returned to Spain I would live in Burgos. The city presented three problems to me. First, this northern part of the Iberian Peninsula is very cold. Second, the people are not very friendly. Third, the clergy and military dominate the city. Because the major part of my university training was received far from the influence of the Franco regime, I was used to a quite different society than the one found in Burgos. Here Franco declared his victory in the civil war and started to impose his dictatorship.

As an immigrant worker in Belgium, I had come in contact with the leftist movements preparing to overthrow Franco. Later, during three years at the Mennonite Seminary in Montevideo, Uruguay, I experienced social struggle brought about by a radical political group called the *Tupamaros*. As I visited countries such as Bolivia, Paraguay, and Brazil, I saw close at hand the human misery caused by the rich who exploited the poor.

When I visited the United States, I found these differences even more extreme. The social contrasts between the U.S. and the other countries I had visited, as well as within the U.S., were so large that the only hope for justice seemed to be through a change. This social change, so needed in all parts of the world where I had visited, seemed possible only through violence. At least that is what the majority of those struggling for change believed and what some practiced. I had even come to sympathize with those ideas.

The repression in Franco's Spain, the injustices done to the immigrant workers in Belgium, the exploitation of the poor in South America—all brought me to believe that the only alternative was the power of violence. It meant applying the law of the strongest. For the weak to become strong, they needed to join forces as an oppressed class and take off the yoke of slavery by any means possible, including violence. Furthermore, the experience in Vietnam seemed to support this idea.

Beyond Violence

When I was 19, I left Spain and the Dominican Order, where I had spent six years, five in the Minor Seminary and one in the novitiate. I wanted to explore the world, learn other languages, and experience a freedom that I hadn't known before. I did not become an atheist, but I left with religious indifference. I was attracted more to Freud's psychology and the existential philosophy of Jean Paul

Sartre and Albert Camus than to the gospel. In the midst of these wanderings, in a providential way, I came in contact with the social work being done by the Mennonites among the immigrants in Brussels, Belgium.

It all started in an unusual way—on a beach close to Barcelona. For the first time in my life, I was by the sea. I had my camera, so I asked a family of immigrant workers from Belgium to take my picture. An Italian man with the Spanish family offered to do it. It turned out that he was the director of social services for foreigners under the Mennonite Board of Missions in Brussels.

One year later, in September 1964, I decided to join the immigration movement to look for work in Belgium, and this man and his family took me in with much love. They were members of the Evangelical Church of Spain, also sponsored by the Mennonites. This church has nurtured many young people who now serve the Lord in Belgium and Spain. In this evangelical congregation I clearly heard the Lord's call to follow him and give him my life.

In that small church in Brussels, the seed was planted that I put into practice in Spain 14 years later when I returned from my travels. That is what I would like to share in this book. I came to realize that I could be a radical disciple for Jesus Christ without being in a religious order. I caught the true sense of a gospel of love and peace, and I could experience real social change taking place without violence.

The Risks of Change

During Franco's dictatorship, Spain was said to set the moral standard for Europe. His death in 1975 brought about many changes that until then were unexpected. One of these changes was democracy. It brought with it political liberty and freedom of speech. It also caused a break with traditional values and a desire to be like the rest of Europe in every way. By joining the North Atlantic Treaty Organization (NATO) and the European Common Market, Spain meant to overcome the mind-set that "Africa begins at the Pyrenean Mountains." Until then Spain and Portugal were considered part of the third world. Today they say, "Now, we are Europeans." Before, those that left Spain to go north said they were going to Europe.

Despite some terrorist attacks, the democratic revolution came about through nonviolent means, although it led Spain to other extremes. For example, it was no longer necessary to go to France to see pornographic movies. Now they could be found in central places of every city. No longer was it necessary to travel to Amsterdam to buy heroin. Even in the smallest towns it could be found at the same prices as in Holland.

Today, Spain is one of the leading countries in Europe for drug abuse. It has one of Europe's highest rates of crime among youth. The media cite "citizen insecurity" as one of the biggest problems for the government. Thefts of cars, business and bank robberies, and other crimes occur daily. Purse snatching, personal assault, rapes, and robberies in homes are reported daily in the press. For example, I just read that half the drugstores in Madrid were robbed last year. The police admit they are overwhelmed. As the number of prisoners increases, so do the jails.

Although there is apparently great social change in Spain, one finds huge problems difficult to resolve. Among those is the case of idle workers. The number of men sitting in bars all day is unbelievable, although it is true that in Spain the whole neighborhood meets in bars to socialize. It is alarming to see that the unemployed come not only from the poorest families, but also from the middle class. Some don't have money to pay for their children's education. Others don't want to continue studying and can't find work either. The problem of unemployment is even more serious among the youth. They are discouraged and without hope for a better future. The situation gets worse all the time.

The Situation of Youth

Young men are more likely to be turned down for jobs in the years before their required military service. No company will risk giving a young man a job because by law it must return that job to him when he finishes his military service. Furthermore, they must pay him during the time he is absent, even if he doesn't work. In reality this hardly ever happens. Since there are few jobs, those with the best potential for profit get them.

A young man without a job spends his time in the bars and on the streets. He goes to the movies where he mainly views sex and violence. At home he can't stand his parents, and his siblings are always interfering with his life. He goes to the nightclubs where he finds his friends and gets into the world of drugs. To have fun, he needs money and even more for a drug habit which is an expensive vice. He cannot induce his family to give him all he needs for having a good time. Once or twice he can borrow from friends but finally he ends up cheating and robbing his family or someone else. I have enough contact with the youth inside and outside the prison to know that this is the case.

New Life in Spain

The moment arrived when I knew it was time to return to Spain. I will try to describe in this book the changes generated by Christlike love and nonviolence. These changes in lives and situations have influenced persons and whole families. All this is a testimony of God's power in a needy world. Above all, it is the proof that the message of Jesus is for the present and applies to situations of social change in our world today.

After being baptized on January 1, 1967, in Brussels, I completed my theological studies in Uruguay. These led me to discover the Anabaptist vision of peace and wholeness in all of life. Afterward, I taught in the European Mennonite Bible School in Bienenberg, Liestal, close to Basel, Switzerland. That is where, in the spring of 1977, I first felt the call to return to Spain permanently.

Through the baptism of the Holy Spirit, I discovered a power from above. This God-given power helped me to overcome deep personal problems and to take steps, through faith, to a renewed ministry. It was through Luke 4:18-19 (quoted at the beginning) that I understood the meaning of the spiritual renewal I was experiencing. The power of the Holy Spirit was not for self-satisfaction but to prepare me better for service to others. From there came my call to dedicate my life to marginal people, the outcasts of society. I was convinced that what psychology or medicine, or even social work couldn't do, God's power could do. God, working through the Holy Spirit in the name of Jesus, the world's only Lord and Savior, could change lives. And that is how the adventure I am going to share now began.

CHAPTER 2

To Preach Good News to the Poor

The Community of Life

"The group of believers was one in mind and heart. No one said that any of his belongings was his own, but they all shared with one another everything they had.... There was no one in the group who was in need. Those who owned fields or houses would sell them, bring the money received from the sale, and turn it over to the apostles; and the money was distributed to each one according to his need."—Acts 4:32, 34-35

The above passage describes the early church in Jerusalem after Pentecost. This experience of living in community, however, has been rejected as a model for the church today. Most Christians view the above example as impractical and invalid, and give greater importance to other experiences that are easier to imitate. Nobody doubts the importance of preaching the gospel or baptizing converts. However, we would do well to give more careful attention to the meaning of this communal manifestation in Acts 2:44 and 4:32. It was the power of the Holy Spirit which led them to such unity and mutual concern that they had everything in common. This spirit of sharing enabled the Jerusalem Christians to respond to the needs of the moment.

We Christians today have the same power and find the same needs in the world. Those of us who have decided to share possessions in common with others understand its importance and the impact it could have on many lives. This is another nonviolent way to change society.

A Small Revolution

It continues to be true that in the world the rich are forever becoming richer, and the poor, poorer. It is said that each day 100,000 persons die of malnutrition while 35 percent of the world's riches are in the hands of professing Christians. What good news can we give the poor? When talking about life in community, we cannot speak only of economic matters. Community also involves the quality of human relationships. This includes the fellowship of persons who, though quite different from one another, live together in harmony.

When trying to bring about important social changes, nothing is more important than style of life and how much money each one uses to live. Communal living has been shown to be much more economical than individualistic living. Economic sharing not only tries to create more economic equality; it encourages a simpler lifestyle than that offered by a society of consumers. In this communal way, progress will not mean that the poor will live like those who are richer, but that all can enjoy the possessions and comforts that are most necessary.

The true challenge Christians can offer the world today is this: We can voluntarily accept a style of life that conserves rather than consumes goods and services. We can renounce the rights that a capitalistic world seems to have imposed on all. That means to renounce "having more" so that others can have what they need. "Having all possessions in common" offers a context where all can live well with less money and be able to take in those who otherwise would live in poverty.

I am not talking here of taking a communal oath of poverty, even if that principle deserves respect. Nor am I speaking of an equal distribution of the gathered possessions of the rich to raise community living standards higher than that of the working class. Instead, it has to do with looking for types of work, production, earning money, and living without luxuries or unnecessary consumption. This will create a pattern of life that does away with the differences between the rich and the poor. Since the doctor and the architect have a greater earning power than the laborer or the maid, the former will renounce overabundance so that the latter will not lack necessities.

Together they will show the world that in Christ they can voluntarily carry out a radical way of life that surpasses communism, which is forced on people. When this happens, the Christian is the real agent of social change that the world needs. And the voluntary acceptance of not owning our own possessions but looking for the common good is the most revolutionary, nonviolent way of creating social change. Communal living is a small society where a small revolution is taking place. If more people could live this way, communal living would become more acceptable in our societies.

Our Experience

Our own experience of community has much to do with what happened in Jerusalem after Pentecost. It has not been the result of thinking and reflection. It came out of the spiritual renewal that occurred among the youth in Burgos about 1975. Some who lived alone started living together on different floors and later these became places for group prayer meetings. When I arrived in Burgos in 1977, the group felt a need to start a community in the country. Here the youth who were in need of rehabilitation from drugs and delinquency could get away from the environment of the city which was doing them great harm. Some of those living in the communities in Burgos joined this new project. The small town of Quintanadueñas, about six kilometers from Burgos, was chosen for this effort.

We had a house here that had been bought by one youth in the community with money he inherited when his father died. The house was in bad shape and the interior had to be almost completely rebuilt. Only the outside stone walls were kept. This house had once served as a meeting place for an evangelical church from Burgos when they couldn't find a place in the city. Several persons had been converted there, and the Lord wanted that house to continue being used for his service. While the house was being rebuilt, the new community moved into a rented house next to the large, old Catholic church that dominated the town. The church tower with its typical nest of storks had become the graphic symbol of the community. In fact, the townspeople are called "storks."

Rebuilding Lives

The beginnings were difficult, but they were full of faith and the power of God. The living conditions were uncertain and dangerous. With the help of a young woman who came from a French community, we learned how to make perfumed candles. At first they were made in jam jars that were collected from the houses in town. The finished candles were sold door-to-door in the city. Little by little the technique of production and packaging was perfected.

We made candles of different bright colors, in various shapes, and wrapped in cellophane. The wrapping had a book-type tag explaining that the community was helping to rebuild lives. Many bought candles as a way to help. The community received most of its income in this way for almost three years. Some sporadic jobs developed and some persons helped us with gifts of money, food, clothes, furniture, and so forth.

During that time, we experienced much hunger, cold, and many material needs. But the Lord was present, revealing himself through signs and wonders—healings as well as conversions, and even daily provisions. Often we received the exact amount of money needed for that day or the food needed by the group, at times as many as 25 persons, and two dogs.

Living together was not always easy but there was great joy and much love for all those who arrived with great needs. At first, young *homeless* people came—those who had no family or had broken their ties with them. Some persons with physical illnesses came, like a young paralyzed woman in a wheelchair. A couple at the point of separation came, as did alcoholics and drug addicts. Persons with psychoses, neuroses, and depression also came.

Soon we found ourselves overloaded with people arriving from all parts of the country, and even other countries, asking for help. Some left with whatever we had in the community purse. Meanwhile, the reconstruction of the house progressed, a symbol of the rebuilding taking place in so many lives that arrived in total ruin.

Difficulties

Things have changed throughout these years. At first the community housed all its residents under one roof. It is now spread out in five homes. One is dedicated solely to rebuilding the lives of criminals, drug addicts, and other marginal people. This ministry has extended to the jail and the streets. One important part of the community is dedicated to evangelization and the building of a community of faith. The faith community is the church or group of believers. It shares one vision and demonstration of the kingdom of God in the city of Burgos.

During these years, many problems have arisen. The external persecution has not been the most destructive. As a community of young people with a pacifist view, most were conscientious objectors. It has not been easy. Burgos is dominated by militarism and traditional Catholicism. But internal conflicts caused most of the damage to the community. This included the withdrawal of some leaders and persons who were apparently highly committed. One of these persons who left the community on bad terms bought a large house in Quintanadueñas, where the rehabilitation program was taking place. Soon afterward, through a lawyer, the members of the community and those in rehabilitation were forced to leave the house and were accused of illegal occupancy. The Lord showed us that we were not to respond in the same way. We should not resort to the courts of this world. So we lost the house that, little by little over a period of three years, we had reconstructed with the help of volunteers and donations.

The house stood empty for two years. It was a large house, rebuilt to fit the needs of the community. It had 14 bedrooms, three bathrooms, and a large living room with a Spanish-style stone fireplace. It seemed an injustice to leave it empty to slowly deteriorate. The town children threw stones through the windows. We suffered, knowing that the humidity would damage the wooden floors. The mice were making their nests there. It was put up for sale through a realtor but couldn't be sold.

Finally, after many problems, we got the money to buy it. It was hard to have to pay for something we had rebuilt almost from scratch. But the Lord reminded us of what he had done for us. He created us, we wandered away through sin, and he had to rescue us at a high price. The death of Jesus was the price God paid so that we could truly belong to him and serve him forever.

The Community as an Agent of Change

That experience taught us how to do things better. We then formed the Christian Association of Communities for the Rehabilitation of the Marginalized (known by its Spanish acronym "ACCOREMA"—for Asociación Cristiana de Comunidades para Rehabilitación de Marjinados). That is the legal name under which we register all properties to this ministry. Besides serving as the legal entity before the government, the association provides access to official services and subsidies. These were of great help to us during a number of years. This legalization gave our work a more serious character in the eyes of the public and in our contacts with police authorities, the judicial system, and other organizations.

The community continues to develop by adding new members. The vision and mission are expanded. But we continue to maintain a sense of family, open to those who are in more need. We don't see the community so much as an end in itself, but as an instrument in God's hands for him to carry out his plan of salvation in this world. I mean salvation in a broad sense, taking into account all aspects of life—material, physical, emotional, and spiritual. Many persons who are poor, abandoned, lonely, declared hopeless by medicine, psychiatry, or social services, have found a home and an answer to their problems.

Today, our church is made up of young people, boys and girls, couples. Had it not been for the community, they would be in mental hospitals, jails, or the victims of suicide. And through them, whole families have been reached. They have regained their faith when they saw God act with his saving power in the life of a member of their family who they thought was lost forever. It often happens that the bad one, the black sheep of the family, becomes the agent for change and ends up being the instrument God uses to bring blessing to many.

The Case of Oscar

This is the case of Oscar Lopez, who comes from a poor conflict-ridden family. He was born in a neighborhood sur-

rounded by delinquency, bad examples, drugs, and prostitution. His father, who died when Oscar was young, had
owned an illegal gambling house. At an early age, Oscar
became involved in the world of drugs, delinquency, and
homosexuality. While being pursued by the police, he left
for the "Legion." This special group in the armed forces
gives refuge to delinquents and young men with problems.
He was looking for adventure and a way of escaping the
authorities.

When he arrived at our community, Oscar had run away
from the Legion. He arrived in a stolen car with a friend
who knew about us and that our town had no police. They
were hoping to cross the border into France because they
were being sought by the authorities. In a surprising way,
when they came in contact with us, they accepted our
challenge to change their lives. They turned themselves
over to the police and had to go to jail.

We helped them in any way we could. We went to visit
them at Melilla, a Spanish city where the Legion is located
in northern Africa. There Oscar spent nine months in a
military prison as punishment. We took him books and discovered that the Bible had become his best companion. He
had left the drugs, alcohol, and even tobacco. He was willing to follow Jesus even in the terrible conditions where he
found himself. In obedience to the Word of God he asked
for and received the baptism of the Holy Spirit in prison,
even before he had been baptized with water. Other members of his family were in prison. Even today, some of them
are still on the road of delinquency.

Oscar returned to the community and not only confirmed his call to serve the Lord but has become an
example of a righteous life. Since his return, he has helped

many to get off drugs and away from the bad life. He was the one who had the vision for our ministry in prisons. Although he has not attended any Bible school, he is an excellent preacher. His wife, Rebecca, has been part of the community since the beginning. Oscar is responsible for the rehabilitation work in Quintanadueñas.

True Spirituality

Over the years, we have learned the importance of several basic principles in community life. The most important are forgiveness and prayer. They are interrelated, for it is difficult to spend time every day in personal and community prayer and to keep harboring resentments toward someone who has offended you. The meals together, the work, and the different community activities are other instruments of change. Our character gets polished little by little by the frictions and problems of living together in community.

In God's family one does not choose one's brothers or sisters. It seems as if the Lord puts next to you the person who will make your weaknesses more evident. It is a constant challenge to change, to transform selfishness and individualism into love and compassion for others. This change is a slow and profound process. There are frequent discouragements and failures. We also discover enormous blessings.

When we evaluate all that has been gained or lost, we can't help but thank God for the community and its transforming dynamics. It is a peaceful revolution in people and in society. When we see how few and weak we are, we are surprised that we have been capable of changing so much ourselves and bringing about so many changes in others in such a short time. In this is seen the meaning of true spirituality: the unconditional surrender to God through service to the brother or sister who is most needy.

"The kind of fasting I want is this: Remove the chains of oppression and the yoke of injustice, and let the oppressed go free.

"Share your food with the hungry and open your homes to the homeless poor. Give clothes to those who have nothing to wear, and do not refuse to help your own relatives."

—Isaiah 58:6-7

CHAPTER 3

To Bind Up the Brokenhearted

The Ministry of Rehabilitation

During the first months of 1970, I had worked for Mennonite Central Committee in the Santa Cruz area of Bolivia, the tropical part of the country. I had an interesting experience close to the little town of Tajibos. Here a project was under way to colonize virgin land taken over by the jungle.

The colonists working there formed cooperatives for better efficiency. Many of the inhabitants in that area were great consumers of alcohol, sometimes in what they called *chicha*, a type of fermented corn. Alcohol had led them to confusion and poverty. Marriage and family life suffered. Immoral sexual conduct caused not only adultery, but illegitimate marriages. Children were born to unmarried mothers, and many fights broke out among friends and families. Besides all this, these peasants suffered exploitation at the hands of those who came from the cities or from overseas to trade with them.

As these persons got to know the true God and became disciples of Jesus, they not only left their bad habits, but their families experienced a true social change. This change affected the whole town and region. The father who changed his way of acting at home improved relationships with his children and his wife. He also improved his economic situation. Further, the fields of those who had become Christians were the best taken care of and the most productive. Their houses were the cleanest and their children the most educated. They were chosen as officials of the cooperatives because the people trusted their honesty and good judgment in the use of money.

I had this same experience in other countries and other cultural contexts, and that is what I am experiencing in Spain now. The message of salvation has a power that changes not only the life of the person who is converted, but also the lives of family members and society. In that way, a nonviolent revolution takes place from the home, the base that has the greatest influence through several generations.

From One Person to the Whole Family

Change the person, and you change the family and society. Based on this principle of peaceful change, our community has been living the experience of change through Christian nonviolence these past few years. This principle has touched individuals and their families and is undoubtedly affecting our society. This is especially needed in Spanish society today, above all, among youth.

Even in the jails, we have seen that as more prisoners

come to know the Lord in a given section of the prison, the life and environment there changes. Where vice and violence once dominated, there is now more peace and beauty. Not only the lives of the inmates are influenced, but also their cells are cleaner, and they are chosen to carry out positions of responsibility.

When we began our ministry, we didn't have any experience in helping people recover from drug abuse or delinquency. Almost without warning, we were challenged with situations for which we had no human response. Nevertheless, the Lord took care of providing everything necessary to confront these problems and find solutions.

I remember one night when one of the brothers brought us a young girl who was involved in prostitution along the streets. She had left the home of her parents because of a fight. She was very poor and seemed to come from a family of gypsies. We cared for her until she was reconciled with her family. This opened the way to help them with their immediate needs. We also prayed for a small child in the home who was almost at the point of death, and later, we learned that the Lord had healed him.

In a similar way, we have received many young people. Some were wandering in the streets. Others were put out by their families. Still others came from mental wards or jails.

Two brothers, Yon and Inaki, came to us from the Basque country, where we received the most calls for help in the beginning. Both were addicted to heroin. Their parents did not know what to do with them. Inaki was a good guitar player. At first, they were surprised that we spoke of Jesus. But they liked the fact that we were what they considered to be a "hippie commune." Yon liked to wear his hair long and wore necklaces. He had to gather his hair with a rubber band so it wouldn't bother him while he made candles. It was amazing how these two brothers became so well integrated into the community, and little by little, they had a personal encounter with Jesus.

Life here was quite different from their life in Bilbao, but, nevertheless, they felt more and more fulfilled. Inaki started spending his free time doing photography. Later, he exhibited his photographs with some success. Yon continued his studies in chemistry. Along with others, they formed a musical group that is now involved in the ministry of praise and in composing new songs that are very uplifting. They convinced their parents that it would be best for the whole family to move to Burgos.

They now live with their parents and two other brothers. Now they are preparing for marriage to two girls they met in the community of faith. The whole family has had a personal encounter with the Lord Jesus, and they are now well integrated into the church. The two younger brothers, Gorka and Aitor, continue the good tradition of music. Gorka now leads a popular group and composes songs that inspire all of us to praise God. This completely transformed family—in spite of their struggles—is one of the many examples we have of the wonderful work of God.

Therapy

What seems difficult to human eyes is not impossible for God. Normally, we are the first to be amazed by the changes. We need to admit that on many occasions, it was not possible to help those who came looking for help. In some cases, all our efforts failed. Such was Salome. After leaving us, fully recovered from drugs and depression, she got together with a friend who took her again down the bad road. She died needlessly from an overdose.

Many have asked us about our approach for change. We have no other therapy except nonviolence and love in the context of discipleship and deep communion. Each individual, from the moment of arrival, is surrounded by care and compassion. No judgments are passed on their previous life; there is no condemnation. Each already has enough grief when they arrive in that state of human degradation. It is true that they have moral responsibility, and they will be taught not to blame others for their situation. The important thing is that they are ready to leave their old life and pay the price of denying themselves and opening up to the marvelous love of God.

Our reception of them is free, for we do not want to mix in money with what is really our way of sharing the good news. The young persons must learn to earn their keep by laboring in our workshops and must accompany us in the dynamic of faith and confidence in God. At first, a more mature person will accompany them everywhere. They are not allowed to visit their family or walk around the city alone. They must attend church activities and explain if they plan any other activity. Gradually, they are given tests of confidence, allowing them to do some things alone and to go out with a bit of money. In that way, we can see how they are responding to the exercise of their new responsibility.

Limits on Acceptance

We have learned that taking in the needy is not a matter of goodwill, of feelings, spontaneity, or improvisation. At first, we received anyone who arrived with any need. The only requirement was that space was available on the floor for them to sleep. We thought of what Jesus said: "I will never turn away anyone who comes to me" (John 6:37b). But the years have taught us that if we have no standards for acceptance, we can do more harm than good.

For example, if our relationship with those who arrived first is tense, the new ones arriving will not be helped. On the other hand, if the number of those needing help is greater than those who can help, good results aren't reached either. At times, the last to arrive have set back others who were well along the road to recovery.

When the number of problem persons is large, power groups form. These end up creating a bad atmosphere through criticism, division, disobedience, and standing up to authority. In that way, they cause burnout in those who were giving them life through love. This does not mean that we haven't committed errors in our actions. But we have learned that the most important thing is to be able to carry out serious and effective discipleship with each person.

Visitors

We have learned the same about visitors and persons who come from other countries. I have been able to make many contacts with Mennonite organizations and churches, and above all, young people in other European countries. When we started this project in Burgos, we made a tour informing others about it and asking for help. We organized summer work camps. We were open to visits from anyone who wanted to spend some time with us. Many were attracted to come since Spain is a tourist country. Students from the Mennonite school in Bienenberg, Switzerland, chose our community as a place to do their practical work.

Through the visits of believers from other countries, we have truly received much help financially and in free labor, besides the enrichment each person has offered. But we must admit that at times too many visitors or too little organization on our part has led to problems.

Sometimes those who came did not find what they expected, and their attitude of service turned into complaints and criticism of what we were doing. At other times, such intimate relationships developed with those in rehabilitation that when the visitors left, problems arose. In some cases, their effort to help a given individual in rehabilitation with money showed discrimination and caused jealousy. And there were destructive sentimental relationships. This taught us to be selective with visitors and to separate work camps from community life and rehabilitation activities.

We learned to limit the number of volunteers to those we can conveniently care for and to strive for an experience that will be edifying for them and helpful to us. Those who come must come with sincere motives and their actions while here must be upright. It is important that they submit to the authorities God has put among us—be it in their work, spiritual life, life together, way of dressing, or personal life. They must not cause a scandal or cause harm to anyone.

Besides the great help we have received in construction, workshops, and everyday life, many who have come have left spiritually renewed and with a call to missions. We know that because of their visit, some have changed their lifestyle and others, as a sign of a greater commitment, have been baptized in their congregations. Some have prepared to better serve God, and others are on the mission fields. The contact with poverty and suffering has made them more sensitive to others and more conscious of the easy and comfortable life they had before. Coming in contact with a more dynamic and sincere faith has challenged them to renewal and to maintain a better relationship with God.

One Day in the Life of the Rehabilitation Community

Every day starts with a call at 7:00 a.m. With the cold climate in Burgos and the chilly atmosphere in the "big house" of the rehabilitation center, it is not easy to get up early in winter. At 7:30, the community prayer time takes place in the large hall with a fireplace. There, close to the fire, one feels cozy and warm. Praise occupies a large part of the prayer time, with joyful songs and even dance. Worship and intercession are also important. Priority is given to prayer for one another, particularly for those who are going through some difficulty. (In summer, we sometimes go out to the fields near the house.)

Each morning there is a time of teaching that tends to be related to pertinent subjects for that moment. Some days there are Bible studies led by responsible believers from the Burgos congregation. We have studied, for example, Romans, James, and teachings about inner healing. This time in the morning provides an important base for the life in community. Breakfast, as well as lunch and dinner, offer privileged times for conversation, laughter, sharing, and communion. It is important for those in rehabilitation to participate in the community meals. It is an essential condition for their integration into the community.

Work is a basic part of our ministry and is carried on for approximately seven hours a day, five days a week. At the present time, it is carried out mainly in the workshops making wooden toys. Starting in spring, some persons work in the garden from which we get much of our fresh produce. In good weather, particularly in summer, some persons reconstruct old houses or build new ones. At the moment, we are building a new workshop.

Working together is good relational therapy and teaches good lessons about life. All who join in the community must work. We consider it a necessary condition for therapy and for remaining in the community. Some cannot work when they first arrive, and that is taken into consideration until they recover. Later, little by little, they start carrying out responsibilities. If it is necessary to spend working hours with someone who has problems, someone may go out for a walk with them or pray with them. The person is more important than things.

The apostle Paul says, "Whoever refuses to work is not allowed to eat" (2 Thessalonians 3:10b). Many of those who come have never worked before. The community therefore helps them acquire values and skills that will help them reenter society when they have been rehabilitated. Those who choose to stay for a while longer to help in the workshops may do so, using their skills to repay what they have received from the community.

Normally, one year is considered the minimum for rehabilitation. In reality, much more time is needed to shape a character that has been deformed over many years. The more time they spend learning, the better, for it will give them more work experience and moral strength to resist temptation once they are on their own. Free time is used in many ways. Often the evenings are busy with church activities, small groups, prayer groups, practice by music groups, visits, or special meetings. Each person is encouraged to take time for personal reading, to develop abilities such as painting, playing a musical instrument, or speaking another language.

On weekends, each participates in the activities of the faith community: the coffeehouse on Saturday afternoon, meetings on Sunday morning, and sometimes special meetings in the evening. During the week, some young people take night courses in general subjects or in specialized ones. Sometimes the believers from Burgos invite them to eat or to go out with them. They go on excursions, travel, or visit other similar communities.

Qualifications of Those Who Work in Rehabilitation

All this work in rehabilitation is possible thanks to those who have unconditionally turned their lives over to the Lord. Much sacrifice and self-denial have been necessary, as well as nights without sleep, much prayer, and many tears. Sometimes we experience the heartache of seeing stubborn ones return to the world of death from which they had come.

One must die to self in order to work effectively in rehabilitation. Our world is one of much unthankfulness and lack of understanding. At times, we even suffer slander and violence, as when it was said that we were drug dealers or CIA agents. We have even been compared to Jim Jones and the "Children of God." We have had doors slammed shut in our faces and indirect persecution that discouraged us in our work. On some occasions, we have been literally hit by irrational people and threatened with death for carrying out our work. For example, a mayor would not let us build, even though we had the legal permits. He swore that he would shoot us if we brought building materials to the lot we had purchased. The Lord taught us to respond with love and nonviolence.

Many of our problems diminished when we became legalized as an association with the name "ACCOREMA." We organized conferences to inform the public about our work. We contacted judges and lawyers who were able to have sentences reduced or to grant freedom from jail for those who lived at our rehabilitation center. The Rotary Club even offered us the help of their professional people, such as the kind architect who has been of such great help in all our construction projects. Business managers have been kind to us by not charging us their commission, as when we bought vehicles, or by giving us free fruits, vegetables, bread, firewood, or other commodities.

Government subsidies were of great help until they got to the point of compromising our principles. Then we had to stop receiving them. We are open to any type of help as long as it respects our Christian character and our style of rehabilitation therapy. Doing social work should not be limited to purely material and psychological aspects, nor should it keep us from sharing our faith with those who recognize their need of salvation.

Although we could say much more about this ministry, we recognize that we have reached this point by the grace of God. As evidence, we see the lives of those who have been transformed and are now agents for transformation. God has given many blessings to those who have consecrated their lives over these years to taking in the poor, the weak, and the outcasts of society. We have responded to the call of Jeremiah in Lamentations 2:19:

> All through the night get up
>   again and again to cry out
>   to the Lord;
>   Pour out your heart and beg
>   him for mercy on your
>   children—
>   Children starving to death
>   on every street corner!

To those who were on the streets suffering, we have opened up the door of our house and our heart. God created a home among us for those without a home. Because "God, who lives in his sacred Temple, cares for orphans and protects widows. He gives the lonely a home to live in and leads prisoners out into happy freedom" (Psalm 68:5-6a).

CHAPTER 4

To Proclaim Freedom for the Captives

The Work in Prisons

The prison in Burgos is considered one of the worst in Spain. Since Burgos is very cold, and the cells were not heated, transfer to this prison was considered a form of punishment. Until recently, this prison was classified as "maximum security" because it housed persons who had committed the worst crimes. The prisoners here had the longest sentences. This was the prison that housed the members of the "ETA," the political terrorist organization that sought to separate the Basque provinces. Some of these fighters were executed in the yards of this prison as a result of the regretfully famous Burgos trial. It tried the terrorists who killed the prime minister of Franco's last government.

Things have changed, and this prison has become one of "moderate security." The sentences are now shorter, and the prisoners are considered less dangerous. Nevertheless, some residents still have long prison terms of more than 30 years. Some improvements have been made in the interior and heat has been installed in some sections. The prison population fluctuates between 500 and 600 persons. Most of them are men. A small section for women can house up to 20.

There are three sections for men. The largest is the "penal" section for those with long sentences. It has prisoners from all over Spain. The "provincial" section is for those with shorter sentences. Here the prisoners are mainly from Burgos, as are those in the "transit" section. It houses those that are supposedly passing through, as its name indicates. In this section, you find those who are held for a few days before being released on probation or under bail. The latter two sections are considered less dangerous. In the penal section one hears of threats and even assassinations.

Rehabilitation in the Prison

To enter the Burgos prison for rehabilitation work and evangelization was not easy. The first visit was to Oscar when he was imprisoned after turning himself in to the police. The change in his life made quite an impression. Later, we went to visit others from the community who had to complete short sentences. Although family members were the only ones legally authorized to visit, we were sometimes allowed to enter because the community was considered their family. When prisoners requested a visit, this call from the inside kept the doors open to us for some time. However, when we knew no one inside, they would not let us in to talk with the prisoners.

We continued in this way for five years. We prayed for the prisoners and for permission to take the message of salvation through Jesus to them, offering them the opportunity to change their lives. We knew that the needs were enormous. We believed that if outside the prison we could be an instrument for God to change the lives of delinquents and drug addicts, we could be instruments inside, as well. We knew the teaching of Jesus about going to those in prison (Matthew 25:36). We knew the exhortation to remember the prisoners as if we were prisoners with them (Hebrews 13:3). We also knew that the prison is a place of pain, loneliness, abandonment, bad habits, and despair. We were aware of the needs inside. Above all, those who had once been imprisoned felt this call. For that reason, we did not give up until we had found a way to enter and work there freely.

We spent many cold hours during the long winter in Burgos waiting at the door, trying to talk to those who could give us the permits. Finally, when we were recognized as a legal association, we presented ourselves with the idea of organizing a series of conferences on the subject of "violence, its causes, consequences, and solutions."

During four consecutive Saturdays, we presented our conference. At the end, some young people that had gone with us gave their testimony of how they had been changed, and with slides, we told about our work. Before we left, we invited those who wanted to change their lives and were willing to participate to join a rehabilitation group. Of the 70 who were present in that room in the provincial section, only five were willing to undertake such an adventure, without really knowing what it meant.

The Prisoners Accept the Challenge

We didn't know quite how to begin our project. We were given a place to meet with this group in the transit section. I remember how cold we were in the small cell where we met. But I also remember how well we were received and how quickly we developed a relationship of friendship and trust during the two meetings each week. We could see the Lord moving with power from the beginning.

Music was an important part of our meetings. The songs most accepted were those composed by Christian gypsies. Some prisoners had guitars, and we taught them the songs. They practiced during the week. We recorded our songs and took them along so they could hear them at other times and learn them. Later, we took recordings of the class sessions in the community. Sharing of the Word in the meetings started leaving its mark in their hearts.

As we continued going to the prison, that huge mass of buildings and walls made of stone became less threatening. As we arrived, it was touching to hear the group singing our songs in the yard. Things changed little by little. In the transit section where we were first allowed to enter, the environment of oppression and violence was slowly transformed into friendliness and tranquillity. The pornographic posters started disappearing from the cells. Each visit, we saw more Bible texts posted next to pictures of beauty and goodness.

Rafa, one of the members of the first group, drew the face of Christ on the whole wall of his cell. One reason we won their respect was that some of the worst criminals believed on the Lord Jesus and had an amazing change in their behavior.

That was the case of Rafa. Despite his wicked-looking face, he turned out to have the heart of a child, as did many others. He started coming to the meetings. He stood sideways in the doorway, ready to leave. It did not take long until he was coming regularly and became one of the leaders. Besides leading the music, he composed songs and maintained order with the rest.

Rafa and José Antonio, who was called Chicho and was sentenced to 30 years, were the two pillars from which we were to build something solid. Five years later, the change in their lives had influenced all sections of the prison. Through the prisoners, we have been able to contact their families, friends, and people from their neighborhoods. It turned out that the majority were from a struggling neighborhood called Gamonal, on the north side of town.

Sentences Are Lowered

Spain, a country with 38 million inhabitants, has 80 prisons with about 22,000 prisoners. Most of them are sentenced for crimes related to the sale or use of drugs. The juvenile delinquents in the streets are mainly "junkies" or heroin addicts. It is common to see young people walking quickly down sidewalks looking in each parked car for a cassette-radio player they can steal. It is hard to find someone who owns a car with a cassette-radio that has not been broken into or had a window broken. On some cars, you can see a little card on the window saying, "Sorry, someone already took it" to let the potential thief know.

The use of drugs can weaken the impact of circumstances in a trial; but because of previous arrests, the sentences are becoming stiffer all the time. Some young people are given up to 100 years or more in prison for the accumulation of many small crimes of theft. It is true that some laws reduce these sentences. Even so, there are young people 18 or 20 years old with 20- or 30-year prison sentences.

Because of our rehabilitation work in the prison, judges have reduced sentences for those on whose behalf we have intervened. That was the case of Rafa who originally had 48 years and finally was left with only 10. Because of good behavior after three years, he was allowed to leave for seven days every 40 days and every weekend. Now he is classified in the third rank and be allowed to go out to work daily from the minimum security section. Rafa is far from the Lord, however, because he has refused to leave certain things of the world. Even though he has momentarily abandoned the teachings of the gospel, however, many changes that occurred in his life still remain. This suggests that our peacemaking influence in the prison goes beyond the number of new believers who continue in the way of the Lord.

Results

I remember Pedro. We had the joy of having him come to live with us when he was released from prison on probation. He started going out with a girl from the community, and eventually they married. Pedro is now working and living a normal life. However, he is also having difficulty with his faith.

We have some young men who have chosen to live at the community in Quintanadueñas when they leave prison because they recognize that they need more time for rehabilitation. They are part of the group from the penal section. They were converted there through the influence of other companions, and now are being prepared to help others.

When they go to other cities, we normally refer them to other evangelical churches with whom we have contact. Here they can continue growing under the leadership of a spiritual authority. In the prison, we prefer to work on discipling in small groups. We have proven that it is better to seek quality rather than quantity. Nevertheless, we organize conferences, movies, music festivals, and other general activities for all those who want to come.

We also have contacts with the minimum security section. Some prisoners here who were in the groups in the prison come to work in our workshops when they come out. This enables them to continue their discipleship training and rehabilitation. The results are not always as good as they should be, but we do not get discouraged because of that.

The size of the team working in the jail has increased over these three years. At this time, we are 12 persons, divided up in groups of two or three, going five times per week. We try to have at least one person in each group who knows how to play the guitar. Music is extremely important. We also carry on a personal relationship with each individual through correspondence and more intimate contacts. These include celebration of a birthday or holiday, such as Christmas. The wedding of one of the team members provided a good occasion to organize pleasant, simple, and life-giving parties in the prison. For those in the prison groups, the rehabilitation community is their home when they go out on leave.

The believers in Burgos who help us in this work are dedicated, devoted, and generous in this ministry—in both spiritual and material ways. The church helps families of prisoners with food or other types of aid. Little by little, all are becoming conscious of this need. It is common to hear a testimony on Sunday of someone who has been released from prison and tells, with great feeling, how his or her life changed because of help from the community.

The Case of José Manuel

Some people ask us if we are not afraid to make these visits because visitors have sometimes been taken as hostages in riots and revolts. The truth is that we feel secure and blessed. We are treated with respect and esteem and can make good contacts, even with those who do not come to the meetings. The prisoners who have been transformed have won the confidence of the rest by their behavior. We cannot deny that they go through difficult times. Often others laugh at them when they read the Bible or listen to Christian songs. But others ask them for literature and show interest. Others observe from afar because they are ashamed to be called pious or seen as weak.

In prison, outward appearances must be maintained at all costs. It is the law of the strongest. There are mafias that put on all type of pressure to prevent any from escaping from their influence and turn them in.

Among the great surprises the Lord has prepared for us are persons coming from other prisons in Spain who have come to know the gospel through other prison ministries. That is the case of José Manuel who came from Cordoba, although he had been contacted by a pastor in Valencia. José was an angel for us, a messenger from God, since he arrived at a key moment in our ministry. Not only did his behavior improve, but besides receiving the baptism of the

Holy Spirit in his cell one night, he continues to be shaped and to shape others. He is involved in a powerful evangelistic ministry, and will soon receive his freedom. In spite of family problems, we hope that he can give his life to helping other companions who are still blind to the light that transformed him.

A Great Challenge

An important aspect of this ministry has been the progress in our relationship with the prison authorities. There were times of great difficulty. Some officials at the prison were bothered by our work. A social worker thought we were getting into his area when we weren't even professionals in the field. In spite of that, the relationships have been encouraging and of mutual respect, particularly in dealing with the administration. They have been able to judge our work by its fruits, and we have sensed their backing and consideration. They have helped us in what is in itself a hard task, and for that, we are very grateful to God. We also have friendly relations with a group of Catholics who visit the prisoners.

Through contacts in other places and countries, we have seen many different situations, and many possibilities for ministry in prisons. What is prohibited in one place can be done with total liberty in another. It depends a great deal on the current laws and even more on the director and administrators at the prison.

The meetings with and materials from Prison Fellowship International, founded by Charles Colson in Washington, have been of much inspiration. We are aware of the good things God is accomplishing in many parts of the world in this complex work in prisons. Certainly, it is difficult to leave everything and take time to visit prisoners. It is even more difficult to form a group of Christians inside the prison. Many problems and situations demand great sacrifice, surrender, and dedication. But many believers are carrying it out, and the fruits show that it is possible and necessary. It is a great challenge, but worth paying the price, knowing that behind it lies a great blessing. The freedom of many captives in prisons may depend on our concern for them:

> Some were living in gloom and darkness, prisoners suffering in chains, because they had rebelled against the commands of Almighty God and had rejected his instructions. They were worn out from hard work; they would fall down, and no one would help. Then in their trouble they called to the Lord, and he saved them from their distress. He brought them out of their gloom and darkness and broke their chains in pieces.
>
> —Psalm 107:10-14

CHAPTER 5

And Recovery of Sight to the Blind

Evangelizing

Spain is one of the countries where the influence of the Protestant Reformation of the sixteenth century did not arrive. Until the recent constitution was approved, Catholicism was the national religion. The influence of Spanish Catholicism has extended to countries in Latin America and parts of Asia and Africa. The Inquisition and the Counter-Reformation had their main backing from the Dominicans and Jesuits, two Spanish religious orders.

The ratio of Protestants to Catholics in Spain is one to a thousand. Many Spanish colleges, universities, radio stations, newspapers, and magazines are in the hands of Catholic agencies that control the world of finance, industry, and the military. The influence, even in the Vatican, of the Opus Dei, a Catholic organization of Spanish origin, is well known. As a result of Franco's victory in the 1936 civil war, evangelicals were terribly persecuted. Because of their faith, they had problems in school, work, and even at the moment of death. In the cemeteries, they had to be buried in special places reserved for the unidentified or those who died by suicide or had been excommunicated.

Things are changing. Freedom of religion was not recognized until recently, but even today, Spain is considered a hard place to evangelize. To this, we have to add the growing materialism of the middle class and the indifference of youth. The youth who have been raised with strict rules do not want to be restricted by a new religion. They prefer to be free, "on their own," as they say. They want to be able to do what they want without having to submit to any moral obligation. One also finds exceptions. Today, many youth and adults experience a spiritual restlessness. This is particularly true because of the sad state of the world and disappointment with politics and work.

More Difficult in Burgos

Besides living in Spain, we are in Burgos. Some say there are liberal, traditionalist, integrationalist, and Burgos Catholics. The later ones form a special category. At this time, Burgos has 250,000 inhabitants. Cid Campeador left from here to counterattack the invasion of the Arabs and their Islamic religion. The Catholic kings received Christopher Columbus here after he discovered America. From here, missionaries left to take the culture and religion of Spain, known as the "mother country," to the new continent.

It is not strange then that every street corner in the old part of the city has one and sometimes two Catholic churches. The religious orders and convents are countless. St. Theresa of Jesus lived in one of them. St. Domingo of Guzman, the founder of the Dominicans, was born in Caleruega, Burgos. According to those knowledgeable in the field, the Burgos cathedral is one of the best examples of Spanish Gothic art. Burgos is probably the only place in Spain where the procession of the rosary of dawn takes the form of a popular demonstration. On huge billboards, next to advertisements for cars, tobacco, and alcoholic beverages, one finds the announcement of the mass and vigils for the day of the Immaculate Conception.

The Legion of Mary, an organization that promotes worship of Mary among the youth, is very active in this city. The most important leaders and managers of this region are representative of those that governed Spain during Franco's time. The wind of change that affected the rest of Spain doesn't seem to have passed through here.

Something happened to us recently that shows the character of the Burguese society and the power of the clergy and Catholicism in this city. We had begun a new evangelistic outreach in a neighborhood to the north of the city. Now we were looking for a place to rent for our meetings. Finally, we found a large one that could be adapted to meet our needs. We spoke to the owner, who operated a building company. We had already given all the information necessary for making out the contract and had bought the necessary cables to install electricity quickly. When they asked what we were going to use the hall for, we told them clearly. When the lawyer from the company found out that we were not Catholic, he said, "Well, we'll have to consult with the authorities."

The next day we were told that we could not rent the

hall. The bank that supported the company was the Savings Bank of the Catholic Church, and they had a say in its administration. This Catholic bank, subordinate to the bishop and the person that accumulates and administers the finances for the clergy, is the only one of its kind in Spain. Its power is greatly felt in the whole region, and it will block evangelical activity such as ours whenever it can.

We have many other examples of the difficulties of moving about freely in daily life. It is even harder to carry out an evangelistic campaign openly. Not long ago we offered a free movie, "Jesus, The Man You Thought You Knew," in the largest theater of the neighborhood. The priests warned everyone in their neighborhood mass, prohibiting any of their members to attend. One person with whom we spoke told us that the priest said we belonged to the Saint John Evangelist sect. (In Spain, evangelicals are known more as "evangelists.")

Youth Respond Better

Besides the established Catholicism, the character of the city of Burgos is closed and cold. Contacts by evangelicals are difficult to make, and confidence is not gained with ease. Maybe it has to do with the climate. This region is the highest part of Spain, more than 1,000 meters above sea level, and is one of the coldest and most mountainous parts of the country.

On the other hand, there are positive aspects. The Spanish nobility is reflected by a sincere and faithful character. The evangelical missionaries who came in great numbers more than 100 years ago went to other parts of Spain, such as Madrid, Barcelona, Alicante, or Malaga. They did not, however, come to this city until about 15 years ago. Those who did come were considered heroes. They dared to defy all the prejudices and powers that dominated this city which had such a bad reputation for evangelization.

The truth is that the beginnings were slow and difficult and few adults have responded to the call to conversion. The people who filled the churches on Sundays and week-days were firmly tied to the rites and traditions of the town. They did not have the spiritual insight to see their need for more of the Lord. The ones who responded most were the young people. Many adolescents—perhaps to break with the demands of their parents or with tradition—approached the Christian communities that began to crop up during the first years of democracy.

Luis Alfredo Diaz, a young Uruguayan artist who came to visit a Finnish missionary, was powerfully used by God about 1975. He came from an evangelical Pentecostal origin and touched the hearts of many young people with his songs. He moved among the Catholics and the evangel-icals and came to be well known in the charismatic move-ment in the country. He had a vision of ecumenism, saw the potential in Spanish Catholicism, and formed groups in Catholic schools and churches. These grew rapidly, and were organized as cell groups and discipleship chains. A unique power impelled them to go out onto the streets us-ing drama, mime, dance, music festivals, and even disguise contests to evangelize. Some lived in intentional commu-nities, attics, and cheap apartments where they had their meetings. There the Lord moved with power.

I remember one called the "catacomb." Many young people crowded into a very small space where they couldn't even stand up because the ceiling was so low.

God's Spirit was strongly evident. There were those who left studies, parents, home, and even fiancées for Jesus.

Difficulties

Around 1980 great opposition developed. Worried parents wrote open letters to the local newspaper asking the authorities to intervene. What sect was this that stole their children and brainwashed them? Who gave the young permission to walk around with a Bible under their arm and to go constantly from meeting to meeting? The religious authorities did not take long to get involved. After some meetings with the leaders, the bishop made this announcement to the press: These communities didn't have anything to do with the true religion. No Catholic should attend or give support to such a deviation.

At the same time, the communities had little relation to other new groups, such as a Baptist and a small Plymouth Brethren group. One reason was the ecumenical character of the movement. The evangelicals in Spain, and even more so in Burgos, doubt the honesty of this type of relationship with the Catholics. Here the Catholics believe that they are the only true Christians.

The ecumenical movement grew until it reached about 300 young people. They were grouped in seven "life and faith" communities with their respective discipleship clusters and spiritual families. They formed a movement of continual evangelistic expansion. They were led by a group of five elders, all between the ages of 18 and 23, under the discipleship and supervision of Luis Alfredo. He was considered the apostle of the movement.

In 1980, everything changed. The external opposition did not do as much damage as the internal division. Problems related to spiritual authority, rivalry among leaders, immaturity and irresponsibility on the part of some, brought chaos to this movement. Although it had been of much inspiration in other parts of Spain and in other countries, many left the movement. Others joined the existing churches, and a few, feeling hurt, dispersed. They looked like a group of friends who were not able to understand what had happened and wanted to relate to each other and learn the lesson. There remained a great fear of words such as *authority, submission, discipleship,* and *spiritual paternity.* The enemy had succeeded in cutting down a young tree, full of very promising fruits. But, was that really achieved? No. Among the ashes a few coals continued to burn. New branches started to grow from this fallen tree and today give testimony to a new awakening.

The Reconstruction

At that time Dennis Byler and his family arrived. They came as a result of a tour we made to communities in the United States. It was organized by Fellowship of Hope, a community in Elkhart, Indiana. We got to know the Bylers and invited them to come and work with the movement in Burgos. That was a little before the work started to deteriorate. Some of the greatest problems with the Catholic Church, and among the elders in the communities, happened while we were on that tour. The arrival of Dennis, Connie, and their children was providential. Their attitude of service, their church experience, and the solid Anabaptist and charismatic foundations in which they had been raised helped to restore the small dismembered group. Like the pieces of a puzzle coming slowly together, each member found a place. We recovered strength, joy, and unity. Today, we again experience that vitality of life that had weakened during almost five years. Above all, we have a new enthusiasm for evangelism.

During this time of dryness in the Burgos community, the rehabilitation ministry in Quintanadueñas and the work in the jail yielded the fruits of conversion. Little by little a precious unity was occurring with the believers renewed by the Spirit in the Baptist Church. Many of them were members of the old communities. They were brought together through the perseverance, faithfulness, humility, wisdom, and tact of their pastor, Roberto Jobe. The problems led Dennis and me to meet regularly with Roberto to pray together about the vision for Burgos. Roberto, recognized for his pastoral authority, intervened so that our community would recognize the ministry Dennis and I carried out as a pastoral team.

Most of the members of our faith community who had not been baptized received baptism during this past year. We now have a beautiful community of about 70 persons, most young couples with children. We also have older couples and new members that come from a variety of backgrounds. Our faith community is made up of two groups. One meets on San Pablo Street, and the other meets on San Francisco Street (formerly a Baptist church). The evangelistic vision of both extended to a joint project known as the Gamonal community.

Gamonal

Gamonal is a problem-ridden neighborhood of 70,000 persons, mainly from the middle and lower classes. There are many fathers without work, many young people on the streets, many homes with problems, and a high level of crime and drug and alcohol addiction.

My wife, Carmen, and I came here in April 1986, together with others from the San Pablo and San Francisco Street communities, to start a new evangelistic mission. Some contacts had already been made here through the prison rehabilitation work. Families of believers from our two congregations had moved to this neighborhood because housing is cheaper here than in the center of the city. Those families had a vision of giving a testimony in this area. The emergence of this project has been providential. We believe this is God's timing. We are already starting to see the fruits of new believers, and the enthusiasm about the Lord is spreading to whole families. The people in this neighborhood are being brought to the Lord through quite different ways.

We have already mentioned how some families were reached when they saw their children quit using heroin and become disciples of Jesus. Others are the families of prisoners who have made remarkable changes that can be understood only through belief in the power of God. We have organized public conferences, movies, musical concerts with mime, and theatrical performances. In the public squares, groups hand out balloons to the children and New Testaments to their parents. Above all, the personal contact with the families and with friends has been our best approach to evangelization.

The reason people believe us when we speak to them about God is this. They see our holistic approach of dealing with the physical, emotional, and spiritual needs, the unity of the whole person. They see how we respond to material as well as social and spiritual needs. The vision of wholeness for persons with problems, and of approaching persons on the margin of society—the poor and the weak—opens the door to their heart. Our concept of evangelization brings solid fruits of repentance to lives that otherwise would never have come to know Jesus as Savior and Lord.

The gospel spreads as we take the homeless in, feed them, help them find work, and give them money or means with which to live. Our friendship, patience, confidence, perseverance, and help with their problems, our disposition to listen and advise on different aspects of their life—all have contributed to the planting of the seed, and at the right time, gathering the Lord's fruits. The work of the Holy Spirit has been crucial in all this. He prepares the road, directs us, refreshes our spirit, and provides the means and creativity. The Spirit's power, seen through the healing and miracles that accompany the testimony and preaching of the believers, is a powerful source of grace and salvation for many.

The Vision

We can expect more from the Lord if we obey His word, improve our lives thereby, and give our best for God's kingdom. Our vision is for only one united church in this city, with the testimony of Christian communities in every neighborhood. Then we will go out to other nearby towns. It is not something we have humanly undertaken. The Lord has led us down this road.

Our beginning gesture of unity among pastors and leaders responsible for each community is becoming contagious to the whole body. A united testimony is the most effective weapon against any attack from the enemy. And we see the fruits: lives transformed by the power of God. Our vision of evangelization includes a concern for peace and social problems and is joined to the manifestations of the Holy Spirit by signs and wonders. This radical discipleship is what the Lord is calling us to.

We would like to live in such a way that not only satisfies us, but also testifies to others that the body of Christ in a city can be united. We will talk about that later on. It has been proven over and over by the growth that occurs that the united testimony of Christians will open the eyes of the blind to their need for salvation. Jesus said so in his parting prayer: "that they may all be one. Father! . . . So that the world will believe that you sent me."   (John 17:21)

CHAPTER 6

To Set at Liberty Those Who Are Oppressed

Creating Jobs

Spain, together with Greece and Portugal, is one of the poorest countries of Europe. In 1987 unemployment reached almost 20 percent of the working population. Large factories were closed. With the industrial changes undertaken by the present government, thousands of persons were left out on the streets.

As companies are modernized, machines replace human beings. This problem mainly affects the young people. Many leave school, and because they can't find work, end up as lawbreakers. The ones hardest hit are the 18-year-olds of military age.

This problem affects the conscientious objectors in a special way. They are considered marginal people, persons with strange ideas who do not want to do what everyone else does. On the other hand, the government does not resolve the request for alternate service. It has been years of unending wait without any sign of knowing how much longer it will last. Unless conscientious objectors to military service form their own business, they will most likely remain idle. The problem is even worse for young people who have a history of drug addiction or a criminal record. This is especially true when they come out of jail.

Burgos is not a great industrial city. The region depends mainly on agriculture (grains) and livestock (sheep). There is also production of potatoes and milk products, such as the famous Burgos cheese. But the farms are in crisis. Many young people are leaving the rural areas to try their fortune in the city. The neighborhood of Gamonal, where we now live, contains families mainly from the rural areas. Some still have their properties in the small towns. They go and come to take care of their houses and gardens there. Those who left the farms increased the unemployment problem in the city.

Since the beginning of our history as a community, we have faced this problem in our evangelistic contacts with youth. We saw the development of jobs as part of our Christian response. It seemed easier to create jobs than to try to find them in a factory.

At the present time, thousands of young people check the newspaper and then visit factories and new stores without finding work because there are few job openings and many job-seekers. For one job alone, 1,000 persons may show up. Many spend years studying and taking exams to gain a position. They go from one city to the next, often far from their home. It is common for 20,000 people to present themselves for exams to fill 400 teaching positions in Madrid. Many obtain their work by "accommodation"; in other words, they are recommended by someone important. Many who finish their studies in law, architecture, education, and other fields, end up doing something quite different from what they prepared themselves to do.

Workshops Develop

The first Christian communities in Burgos were made up mainly of students. The problem of employment occurred above all in the rehabilitation center. Those of us who started that venture set out on a financial adventure. The Lord was the one who helped us come out ahead. Prayer and imagination had to be put into practice, for we received no help from the church or the state that might have guaranteed a regular income. Because of the need for employment, the candle workshop, which maintained the community the first years, was developed. Spanish society seldom uses candles to decorate, although they are used in the Catholic churches for religious purposes. Therefore, the huge number of candles we sold is still surprising. We had no doubt that the Lord was backing up his mission through this simple task that didn't require much investment.

As the community grew, its needs also grew. The rehabilitation center wanted to improve its housing facilities and the food supply was very uncertain. We now had couples with children. They needed to live in houses different from those where the rehabilitation work took place. The children had not chosen this lifestyle, and living among outcasts and derelicts was a source of great tension. This meant more expenses and we needed to look for other areas of work that would provide a better income.

When we visited a community in Basel, Switzerland, we discovered the possibility of making wooden toys. They let us copy our first patterns and generously helped us to get our first supplies. The machinery was simple and the whole process quite manual. We specialized in decorative inlaid puzzles (marquetry), cut with a small electric saw and handpainted. Later, we continued with more complicated models and started making instructional materials that were widely accepted in schools and day-care centers. The machinery, as well as the production, needed to be increased all the time. A catalog was printed and others soon followed. We tried to improve the presentation each time new things were added. Even though we were not experts in this type of business, the Lord directed us in developing a company that is legally able to make and sell materials on a large scale.

Today, we continue to move forward against greater challenges, but without reducing the quality of the finished product. We have introduced new techniques, such as making silk screens (serigraphy) for painting and using a compressor for spray varnishing. And we have a vision of growing even more. Our final objective is to make this business the economic base of the community, besides helping to rehabilitate people and providing paid work for those who do not have it.

Offering Alternatives

It is especially important to offer jobs to those who come out of prison. The Lord has shown us that we should not only take to prisoners the good news offering them a better life, conversion. We should provide a means for them to live decently and to learn those values they don't know or have rejected because of problems in society. Work teaches those who are being rehabilitated about obedience, order, and discipline. They value their work as they value what they have made with their own hands. They learn what it means to provide for their needs and those of others. When they leave the community they are no longer a burden, but a help. As the apostle Paul says: "Let the thief no longer steal, but rather let him labor, doing honest work with his hands, so that he may be able to give to those in need" (Ephesians 4:28, RSV).

From their experiences while in the community, those who leave can find work and know how to respond to the demands put on them. Some have been able to develop their own companies or find jobs because of what they learned. These include a builder, a photographer, a serigrapher, and a distributor of instructional materials for preschoolers. The believers from the community of faith have been able to develop jobs by forming companies that as a general rule are going well. Two young families formed a company to clean buildings and offices. They now employ eight people. One brother has formed a company to lay pipes. Another developed an electrical company. Still others work as furniture-makers or as masons. Some would like to make music their profession but that is difficult.

In this search for jobs we have learned to help one another. This has been a subject of prayer and faith but also of putting together our resources. As James 2:15-17 says,

> My brothers, what good is it for someone to say that he has faith if his actions do not prove it? Can that faith save him? Suppose there are brothers or sisters who need clothes and don't have enough to eat. What good is there in your saying

to them "God bless you! Keep warm and eat well!"—if you don't give them the necessities of life? So it is with faith: if it is alone and includes no actions, then it is dead.

Ethical Principles in Business

Two young people in our community of faith started a business of video filming and photographic reports. They formed a cooperative with others who were not Christians, but things did not go well. The same thing happened with a barber shop and a clothing store. We recommend that when forming companies, Christians associate only with committed Christians of the same faith. We believe Paul's teaching about not being mismated with unbelievers (2 Corinthians 6:14) still holds true. But we recognize that this principle is not always easy to apply.

We believe that even though we ourselves need help, we should also help others. We have therefore tried to help Christians from other communities that are poorer than ours. We send them tithes and offerings to help them start companies and buy machinery and vehicles that will help them advance. It is doing for them what others did for us. That was the case of a community of Zaragoza. We lent them money without interest, and made a donation, so that they could buy an offset printer and an electronic type-writer to print a magazine and do jobs for pay. We trust the Lord, and believe he will continue to provide ideas and means for creating more jobs. There are already plans to start a day-care center, a shoe store, and a workshop to repair leather and plastics.

As we work at providing jobs for the unemployed, we plan and carry out training sessions with them. These deal with the biblical concept of work, professional ethics, and the relationship between forming companies and building the kingdom of God. We deal with such questions as: To what extent is profit the main criteria of a Christian company? What should be the relationship between the employee and the employer in a Christian company? How can our companies serve to communicate the gospel and build the church?

We consider it important that each individual work to earn his or her own room and board. We think it is important for everyone to be responsible for God's work by giving a tithe and an offering to the congregation. We teach them to be conscious of the needs of others, to give money personally to help them.

Work is necessary for the psychological and spiritual development of every human being. Even though some consider it a curse, we need to recognize that God entrusted work to a man and a woman before the Fall. Work dignifies the one who does it. It is an expression of the person, a reflection of the image of God, the Creator. Human beings need an occupation. They need to see the labor of their hands, to feel useful and needed, to value themselves by what they do. The book of Proverbs is full of warnings against laziness and of praise for the worker.

Someone has said that work is a vitamin for the soul, and when it is absent, the person suffers from moral rickets. We have seen some fall into depression, neurosis, and a desire to commit suicide when they find themselves without work. Sometimes, just to be doing something, they start doing things that are not constructive.

Our Responsibility

The modern, mechanized world takes away a person's

opportunity to work. When this happens, society ends up paying for the damage through psychiatric hospitals, prisons, and centers for the unemployed. It is well known that those who retire and don't do anything die early. They deteriorate more easily with idleness than if they could continue their occupation longer. In our rehabilitation center we have seen that the hardest days are holidays and weekends when there is no work. Behavioral problems increase during these times. Some persons fall into loneliness. They develop patterns of bad thoughts and harmful activities because they don't know how to use their free time. Rest and recreation are also important. We put great emphasis on the joy of a party. We often celebrate birthdays and special happenings with all types of creative and recreational activities.

Many young people look for all kinds of reasons for not working and for "having a good time." To them, this means going to the bar, the theater, the nightclub, or the street with friends. As a result, they do not know how to work. For that reason, when we tell them the liberating good news of salvation through Jesus, we must teach them to work and provide jobs for them.

On the other hand, many are oppressed by their employer at work. Work on an assembly line can be inhuman and discouraging. More and more is demanded without providing for the needs of the worker. We must seek justice. But we have confirmed that for most, it is worse to be without work than to be working under difficult conditions. That is why, in order to free the oppressed, it is necessary to provide for the important need of meaningful work.

The person who has a paying job has a great privilege

that not all can reach. Although some don't work because they don't want to, many want to and can't. For these, we need to find jobs. That is part of their salvation. If I have a job, I feel responsible to help others find one, too. Since the kingdom of God is the most important thing in my life, my responsibility as a Christian is to respond to the basic needs of others. And one of the most important needs is work, to have what is necessary to live, and help others. That is what the apostle Paul said: "I have shown you all things that by working hard in this way we must help the weak . . ." Acts 20:35a.

CHAPTER 7

To Proclaim the Acceptable Year of the Lord

Peace and Unity

Jesus told his disciples, "Peace is what I leave with you; it is my own peace that I give you. I do not give it as the world does. Do not be worried and upset; do not be afraid" (John 14:27).

True peace is possible only when we find him. Our differences don't need to create walls of separation or cause us fear. Because of him we are one. He is our peace (Ephesians 2:14). The unity we want to see between divided countries, and the world peace we desire, should first be lived among Christians. We should learn to live in peace in our communities and in our churches, in the city and in the country.

The task of unity and peace has required much energy and dedication at various levels. I am not talking about handing out tracts on Christian pacifism. Unity and peace have to do more with giving a testimony of how those who believe in the gospel of peace have put their convictions into practice at a local, national, and international level. Our pacifist doctrines are useless if not applied at all levels, starting with our personal life.

I am not going to mention ways we can solve our internal or family conflicts. Rather, I want to show how we have come to live in unity and peace among Christians and how our testimony through our actions ripples through our society. The problem of nuclear war and the arms race worries us and we believe that Christians should not teach "death to the enemy" as the military institutions declare. Our duty is to work for unity and peace.

Experience in Unity

Through the years, it has been clear that God's will for Burgos was the unity of all born-again Christians. The will of God, our Father, is to have one great family in this world with many children who are similar to Jesus. The relationship among God's children should be the same as that of the Father and his Son Jesus. For that we have the Counselor, the Unifier, the Holy Spirit. The Spirit leads us to all truth and reveals to us what Jesus did for us to bring us his unity and his peace.

This task of unity has not been easy. Little by little we are reaching it, and we realize that God is blessing this plan. In spite of divisions and difficulties in the past, today we have three communities in the city and are reaping the good fruits of unity and peace. We move freely from one congregation to another for meetings, celebrations, and other activities. We share part of our finances in joint evangelism projects and in support of the rehabilitation ministry. For quite a while we have been having a monthly joint worship meeting. We share common teaching, a type of congregational Bible school. It has started to function in a modest way with one course on the Old Testament to be followed by others. Its purpose is to train Christians and leaders at a local level.

At times, some who have gone to school at other places were of no help to us when they returned. We do not deny the possibility that some are able to train at more qualified centers of study, but local training is a priority for us. For that reason, God has given us persons with the gifts for teaching. Still others are preparing for that task. It is a common practice for us to share in our various ministries. The weekly meeting of pastors is a testimony of the unity at the level of spiritual authority.

One beautiful and practical proof has been the development of the new community in the Gamonal neighborhood. About eight persons from each of the two established congregations were sent as active members, with their tithes and gifts, to support this new community. These two congregations are not large. One had 80 members and the other 120. They have learned, though, that sharing even what they need—sending out the best they have—has brought blessings.

We do not overlook unity with other Christian brothers and sisters as long as the unity is in Jesus. Unfocused cooperation can cause more conflict than it resolves. There are different levels of unity. We know from experience the limits in working with members of the Catholic Church so as not to cause confusion for born-again believers. We finally had to stop having the eucharistic celebration that we used to have in retreats with members of the

Catholic Church. Sharing in this symbol of unity really led to more division.

Another divisive experience with our Catholic friends occurred at a prayer meeting in a prison. We had to end this cooperating ministry because some of them insisted on singing songs about and praying to the Virgin Mary. We cannot forget that love should be accompanied by truth and that our love for peace and unity cannot contradict the biblical foundations of our beliefs. And from that standpoint, we cannot accept many Catholic practices for the sake of unity. On a personal level, however, we maintain good relationships with some Catholic Christians. We do go to some Catholic communities to use their retreat centers. We carry out activities with Catholic groups as long as these do not contradict our faith and don't lead us to do what the Bible does not support. We wish that even with Catholics, as well as other denominations, we could feel the communion in the Spirit and live in the Lord's peace. So that "there shall be one flock, one shepherd" (John 10:16b, RSV).

Concrete Steps

Through a bond of love, we have come to form a chain-like link with seven communities in Spain, two of which are Catholic. Here are a number of the things which join us together:

- The renewal of the Holy Spirit
- The concern with and action on issues of peace
- A practical commitment toward the poor and the marginal folks
- The reality of the church seen as a vision of community

- •Recognizing the need to carry out the task of evangelism
- •Building the body of Christ through discipleship, stressing separation from the world in holiness and discipline
- •Unity of converted Christians

Since about ten years ago, this cooperation has led us to have joint meetings of leaders and to have a joint fund for expenses to annual encounters and visits. We look for unity in aspects of doctrine and life. We acknowledge each other's ministries by inviting one another to minister in each of the locations. We listen to the advice of the members, even when we do not ask for it, and are united as leaders when members transfer from one community to another.

These ties of unity with various communities and congregations all over the country keep growing in number and meaning. With some we are more united because of similar ministries or doctrines. Some work more with marginal people, and we have more contact because of this. In some cases the unity is greater because of the evangelical background that makes us feel a greater communion. That is true as well for those who define themselves as Catholics.

Peace Brings Unity

One important aspect of this unity is the matter of peace. The majority among us are conscientious objectors. Some are specialists in pacifism and nonviolence. In this matter we are united with European groups, as well as with the "peace church" movement. Most of the intentional communities in Europe, whether Mennonite or not, are pacifist. We maintain contacts through meetings or tours.

The international work camp in Burgos is also a good point of unity in a practical sense. Culture and language differences are overcome by a spirit of unity, love, and peace. Our vision is that the body of Christ will overcome races and boundaries. Based on a strong biblical foundation, we work toward unity and peace among Christians and a peace for the world arising out of our local situation. This evidence of unity gives authority to our words. It is not possible to speak of unity and peace with impact and conviction if it is not being lived locally. True, we all live with the hope of what can still be done. But the gospel is God's power for those who believe and this power is the only one capable of creating the conditions necessary to put unity and peace into practice.

Many other groups, communities, and churches—evangelicals as well as Catholics—are concerned about the unity of the body of Christ, peace among Christians, and peace in the world. I have just received a letter from the Evangelical Conference of Spain making a call for unity of the Lord's people in Spain. The Spirit is moving in other cities to bring about unity of Christians. We have heard of churches in Cordoba in southern Spain, Valencia in the east, Bilbao in the north, and others that are walking united.

Youth with a Mission, an organization active in evangelism and social service to the needy, has a special ministry of worship and presentation of the gospel through music and drama. They are working with evangelicals, as well as Catholics, to be a bridge and to serve God among all the believers.

An ecumenical movement called "Taize," well known among the youth of Europe, is trying to unite Catholics and Protestants through prayer and meetings. They are concerned for the poor and for world peace. The movement to form communities tends to unite Christians in their commitment toward peace. Such communities create pockets of hope for unity and peace in the whole body of Christ.

The movement for peace is equally important in the whole world, even among non-Christians. There are those who speak out for peace, not because of religious convictions, but because of moral or ecological reasons. This is true above all because of the danger of nuclear war and the increased rate at which "star wars" technology has advanced. We have experienced this type of unity in Spain in our struggle to make conscientious objection legal.

I remember even in Franco's time, some secret meetings held in a monastery in the French Pyrenees. Young people from all parts of Europe met there with Christians from Spain. They told of persons in prison because they opposed military service for reasons of conscience. Among those attending was a group prepared to present a project on alternate service. They started to carry it out in Hospitalet, a poor neighborhood in Barcelona, until they were taken to prison. Soon after that, Franco died and the law of conscientious objection was recognized.

This law is not enforced today and is questionable because of its restrictive nature. This same unity exists, however, among different groups of conscientious objectors in Spain trying to find a solution. At this time, several conscientious objectors are in prison because they declared their position during their military training. We show our solidarity with them.

In some cases, this commitment to peace has been an opportunity for evangelism. The announcement of the arrival of the Messiah was accompanied by a proclamation of angels: "And peace on earth to those with whom he is pleased" (Luke 2:14). Among the pacifists who do not identify themselves as Christians we have found many men and women of goodwill. They are often open to the good news of the Messiah, Jesus Christ. They represent opportunities for evangelism.

Unity Brings Peace

In the same way that concentrating on peace brings unity to pacifists, the search for unity is also a condition for peace. And it does not mean uniformity, but real unity— the kind that exists between the Father, the Son, and the Holy Spirit, each with their own functions and personal identity.

Seeking unity among different Christian groups in a city means taking steps toward peace. Only the Spirit of God can help us to overcome barriers that separate us. Just as an overflow of water can unite ducks that were separated by fences, so is it when the Lord's Spirit overflows in us—true unity is reached. It is the acceptable year of the Lord, the sabbatical or jubilee year. All debts are pardoned, slaves freed, properties returned to those who had to sell out of necessity. The joy of reconciliation, unity, and peace is enjoyed.

Only the Messiah, Jesus, the "Prince of Peace," can bring about the acceptable year of the Lord or the unity and true peace that pleases God. "His royal power will continue to grow; his kingdom will always be at peace"

(Isaiah 9:7). He is the only Lord of peace that can give you peace at all times and in all ways (2 Thessalonians 3:16). Those who find their hope in him are united through his Spirit in a bond of love and peace that only he can give. Our task is to seek peace and pursue it (Psalms 34:14). Search for unity that brings peace. For where there is unity, where brothers live together in unity, something wonderful happens: "There the Lord bestows his blessing, even life forevermore" (Psalm 133:3, NIV). For that reason, the apostle Paul says, "Do your best to preserve the unity which the Spirit gives by means of the peace that binds you together" (Ephesians 4:3).

Epilogue

You have just read a testimony. Through a series of concrete experiences you have seen how the gospel acts as an agent of change through love and nonviolence. In Burgos we are not doing any extraordinary thing. We preach and live the gospel and this has a practical effect, causing positive changes in our society.

The gospel we live and preach is the same one Jesus lived and preached in the first century in Palestine. Jesus, filled with the Holy Spirit, started his ministry of salvation by forming an intentional community with a group of disciples. Judas, who betrayed him, was also among them. Judas had the responsibility of the community finances and stole from this common fund (John 12:6). In this first Christian community, Jesus united such opposing Jews as a nationalist revolutionary Zealot with a publican (public official who had sold out to the Roman Empire). He reconciled such different personalities as an explosive Peter and an even-tempered John.

The ministry of Jesus fulfilled the prophesy in Isaiah 61. Jesus applied this passage to himself at the beginning of his ministry in the synagogue in Nazareth (Luke 4:21). His task was to rehabilitate the social outcasts, heal the sick, and free all that were oppressed by the devil (Acts 10:38). He fed the hungry and raised up the dead, spiritually as well as physically. Mary Magdalene, a prostitute, was converted and became one of his main helpers. She, with other women healed of evil spirits and infirmities (Luke 8:1-3), traveled with him and his disciples to many cities. Jesus had a special preference for the small, the weak, the poor, those who cry and suffer, those who labor and are heavy-laden. To these, he offered rest in himself (Matthew 11:28).

In his parables—like the Good Samaritan (Luke 10:30-37) or the Lost Sheep (Matthew 18:10-14)—Jesus invites us to take care of the fallen and those who need help, those who are lost and need salvation. Jesus upheld all the Law and the Prophets. He said no other commandment was as important as loving God with all our strength and our neighbor as ourselves (Mark 12:30-31). And as if that wasn't enough, the Lord asked us to love one another as he loved us (John 13:34). And what does it mean to love each other as he loved us? It means to forgive, be willing to suffer for each other, give our life even for those who do not love us, for our enemies and those who persecute us (Matthew 5:44). Because God is that way—kind to the ungrateful and the selfish—we need to be that way also (Luke 6:35-36).

Concerning work, Jesus taught us through the parable of the laborers in the vineyard (Matthew 20:6) that the Lord of the vineyard does not like to have laborers who are idle all day. Jesus implies what Paul says later: "The laborer deserves his wages" (Luke 10:7; 1 Timothy 5:18). Jesus does not add anything new on the subject. He takes for granted the teaching in the Old Testament concerning dignity of human beings and their responsibility to earn their keep and be capable of helping others. Following the scriptural revelation, Jesus did not only address himself to the spiritual needs but also to the material and social needs of the human being.

We Christians have to share that same vision and that same practice. Our congregations and communities will have to respond to the challenge presented by the problems in our society. To give the good news to the poor and to heal the brokenhearted our homes need to be open. Our congregation needs to assume the responsibility of opening centers of rehabilitation. Those will become centers for healing. For such ministry, we don't need many resources but a willingness to serve, a spirit of sacrifice, and a heart open to the suffering of others.

There are prisons everywhere and, as Jesus said, "The poor you always have with you" (John 12:8, RSV). To preach freedom to the captives and to free the oppressed, we cannot offer them only the gospel of salvation for their soul. Rather, all their life—spirit, soul, and body—has to be touched by God's power. Giving good news to the poor is to teach them the truth and give them the means for a social change. To give sight to the blind is to open their eyes to spiritual realities that they cannot see because of their sin. It is also to return to the joy of life those lost in the darkness of despair because of psychological, physical, and economic problems.

You, of course, have your own story to tell. But maybe God has something more reserved for you. There are people who need you right where you are. How many are crying without you knowing it? You, together with your community or congregation, can help them. The fact that others don't do it does not justify your inaction. Your life can be an instrument in God's hands if you let God use you as he wants. And God wants to. You may have to give up many things you like—your comforts, your isolation—for this to happen. Are you willing to leave anything to follow God?

There is no greater joy than doing God's will. The apostle Paul says that God's will is that all should be saved and come to the knowledge of the truth (1 Timothy 2:4). That is your responsibility as well as mine. Are you willing to be used by God as an agent for change in the lives of many through love and nonviolence? That is to live the gospel. Are you willing to be sent to those who suffer the consequences of sin, as Jesus was? If that is so, Jesus also says to you, "Receive the Holy Spirit" (John 20:22). And when you go out in the name of Jesus to preach the acceptable year of the Lord, you can go out trusting in him, knowing that the Spirit of the Lord is upon you.

The Author

José Gallardo ministers in churches and intentional communities in Burgos, Spain, as well as in some other countries of Europe. He was born in Albacete, Spain, and raised Catholic. At the age of 11, he attended a Catholic seminary of the Dominican Order.

After completing high school, he went to Belgium as a migrant worker. Here he met the Mennonites through their relief and social service activities among Spanish migrants. After he became a member of the local church, he received a call to prepare for full-time Christian service.

From 1968 to 1970, he studied at the Mennonite seminary in Montevideo, Uruguay, and during 1971-72, he attended Goshen Biblical Seminary in Elkhart, Indiana. Later, he completed his theological studies in Brussels with a thesis on discipleship and nonviolence.

While in South America, he worked with inmates in the prisons of Montevideo, served Mennonite churches in Uruguay and Argentina, and worked with Mennonite Central Committee workers in the region of Santa Cruz, Bolivia. Later, he assisted migrant workers in Europe, taught New Testament and social ethics part-time at the Bienenberg Bible School in Liestal, Switzerland, and worked as a delegate of the International Red Cross.

In 1975, he was ordained as an itinerant preacher and teacher at a European Colloquium of the Mennonite Board of Missions and as a part-time pastor of the Spanish Mennonite Church in Brussels.

In 1978, he returned to Spain and joined a renewal movement among young people in Burgos. In the nearby village of Quintanadueñas, he helped to start a community of rehabilitation for drug addicts, delinquents, and outcasts. From here, he continues an itinerant ministry among churches and small fellowship groups in Spain and other countries of Europe.

In 1985, he married Carmen Ochoa, and they moved to the problem-ridden neighborhood of Gamonal. Here they started a new congregation related to the prison and rehabilitation ministries.

PEACE AND JUSTICE SERIES

Edited by Elizabeth Showalter and J. Allen Brubaker

This series of books sets forth briefly and simply some important emphases of the Bible concerning war and peace and how to deal with conflict and injustice. The authors write from a perspective rooted in the Anabaptist heritage of the sixteenth century. This includes a holistic view of the Scriptures as the believing community discerns God's word for today through the guidance of the Spirit. Some of the titles reflect biblical, theological, or historical content. Other titles in the series show how these principles and insights are lived out in daily life.

1. *The Way God Fights* by Lois Barrett.
2. *How Christians Made Peace with War* by John Driver.
3. *They Loved Their Enemies* by Marian Hostetler.
4. *The Good News of Justice* by Hugo Zorrilla.
5. *Freedom for the Captives* by José Gallardo.
6. *When Kingdoms Clash* by Calvin E. Shenk

The books in this series are published in North America by:

Herald Press
616 Walnut Avenue
Scottdale, PA 15683
USA

Herald Press
117 King Street, West
Kitchener, ON N2G 4M5
CANADA

Overseas persons wanting copies for distribution or permission to translate should write to the Scottdale address listed above.